T0210003

Cash's Flight Plans & Adventures

TOIRESA FRAZIER

WestBow Press books may be ordered through booksellers or by contacting:

WestBow Press
A Division of Thomas Nelson & Zondervan
1663 Liberty Drive
Bloomington, IN 47403
www.westbowpress.com
844-714-3454

ISBN: 978-1-6642-1682-2 (sc)
ISBN: 978-1-6642-1684-6 (hc)
ISBN: 978-1-6642-1683-9 (e)

Library of Congress Control Number: 2020925395

Print information available on the last page.

WestBow Press rev. date: 01/20/2021

WestBow
PRESS®
A DIVISION OF THOMAS NELSON
& ZONDERVAN

To my son, Cash. I am honored God gave me you.

And now abide these three, faith, hope and love, but the greatest of these is love.

—1 Corinthians 13:13

ForeWord

Cash was considered the official or unofficial greeter at the Ontario airport. He knew which airplanes were flying, who was piloting them, and, of course, where they were coming from. The cool kid in a flight suit was personable and smart, with an incredible passion for aviation. He made a point of getting to know each person transitioning through the area. It was at the airport where he was most comfortable and in his element, which was immediately obvious by his smile when welcoming each pilot. Those of us in aviation meet a lot of kids. Most admire the airplanes and their capabilities, but none are quite like Cash. Cash was special—a happy soul in a league of his own, who received his wings too soon.

Parker Lucas
RJ-85 Captain
AeroFlite, Inc.

Hi, I'm Cash Troyer. Thanks for picking up my book about adventure in aviation! I love adventures of all kinds, but my favorite is right here at the airport, around all the airplanes. Some of you may have family members who are pilots or who work in the aviation world, and some of you may not have flown on an airplane yet. Either way, I'm glad you are here.

My interest in airplanes and helicopters started when I turned three years old. My granddad built a pedal plane for me. At first, I could barely reach the pedals to make it go, but before long I was zipping around on the ground, and my love for planes was airborne. It's important to find something exciting and interesting and even adventurous to learn about and be a part of in some way. What is something you love to learn about and do?

My granddad has the fixed base operation at the airport, or FBO for short. The FBO sells fuel to aircraft and rents hangar space for planes and helicopters and offices for businesses. Some FBOs have mechanics shops and flight schools. When people are traveling to another destination, they can land here at this airport refuel their airplane or helicopter, stretch their legs, and use the restroom, and if they want to get lunch, they can use one of Granddad's courtesy cars to go into town. Did you know that every airport has a identifier? The identifier is a short version of the airport name. Our airport identifier is KONO. Four letter codes identify the region in which the airport is located. The three letter codes for the larger airports are most common to travelers. If you like being a detective, look up the airport that is close to you and see if you can find out what its four-letter identifier is. Write it down here, and then you won't forget it. _____

My pedal plane is painted just like my granddad's plane. I park it next to his in the hangar and when he pulls his out in front of the FBO, I bring my plane out and park beside him.

I bet you are wondering about the word *hangar*. It's like a garage for airplanes and helicopters but with extrawide doors so that the wings and rotors will fit. Most hangars are at the airport, but you can also find them at airparks. Airparks are like subdivisions created for pilots. I watch the other pilots work on their airplanes, adjusting and washing parts of the planes, so I do the same with my plane.

When I started going to the airport, there was an old NASA airplane on the field that had at one time been used to simulate the space shuttle landings for astronauts to practice with. This was perfect for me because I had a NASA suit, so I could pretend that was my ship and I was flying to the moon and would be back before dark.

When I was little, I learned to ride my bike at the airport. Granddad took the training wheels off my bike, and I was hoppin' mad about that situation. But one of the pilots working with a helicopter told me that he didn't let his little girls have training wheels, and they were younger than me and could both ride their bikes. Well, once I knew that, I had to get the hang of it pretty quick.

The pilot, André, also told me he would have me riding my bike in ten minutes. I doubted his confidence, but my back was against the wall, so I jumped on it. It turned out that André,

who was from Switzerland, knew what he was talking about. He was a skilled pilot who had flown all over the world. How cool was it that we would meet in America just so he could teach me to ride my bike?

Once I could ride my bike everywhere, Mom informed me that in fact I could *not* ride my bike everywhere. There had to be boundaries. The storm drain in front of the hangar was the limit for the longest time. I'm glad I grew out of that. Now I'm free to roam about because I have a better understanding of what is going on with the traffic on the tarmac, and I go around the busy areas. A tarmac is the parking area for aircraft, and a taxiway is the road that aircraft use to get to and from the runway. The runway is where airplanes take off and land.

Some pilots equip their tail-dragger aircraft with big tires so that they can land on backcountry strips. A tail-dragger has two tires attached to the main body of the plane, with a smaller tire back under the tail of the plane. These types of planes were designed for taking off on shorter runways and going to backcountry strips. They fly slower than jets, and you can get closer to the mountains to see deer, elk, and high mountain lakes. The big tires help the landings be smoother and keep the aircraft from getting damaged by rocks and uneven ground.

Granddad takes me in his Cessna 182 to practice flying. It's easier to learn because I'm sitting right beside him. The Super Cub is a tail-dragger, so I sit behind him; I can't see everything he is doing to make the plane fly. There are a lot more gauges and switches in the cockpit of a plane than there are in a car or a truck. One day I'll understand them all.

When I was six years old, I got to take my first ride in a helicopter. Mr. Butler is a local rancher, and he uses his helicopter as equipment for his ranch work. When his cattle hear him in the helicopter, they know it's time to move to a new pasture. He rounds them up gently and gets them pointed in the right direction, and off they go. He stays behind them so that they know not to turn back.

Do you know what else he can do with his helicopter? During the summer, when the cherries are close to being ripe, they might split open and ruin the crop if they get wet. So Mr. Butler flies above the orchard to move the air and dry the cherries.

Really big helicopters can haul water to fires, haul heavy cargo, or set towers up. Smaller helicopters can haul sick passengers to hospitals, fly people to do surveying, and rescue people from mountains or boats.

Summers at the airport are my favorite. It is so exciting to watch big helicopters coming in on their way to fight fires. Sometimes, if we have a fire that is close to our airport, the big helicopters stay at our airport. The biggest helicopter we get in is the AirCrane® helicopter. It has a snorkel, which is like a big hose at the bottom of the aircraft that sucks up water into a holding tank. Then the helicopter transports the water right to the fire. The firefighters can get the water from lakes and rivers and ponds if they need to.

When I could still fit in my pedal plane, I had a flight suit to go with it. When I saw that the fire crew wore helmets while they were flying, I used my ski helmet so that I matched them. Let me tell you—those helmets are hot in the summer! Our airport is an aerial wildfire base during the summer, and that means we see the single engine air tankers, or SEATs for short. The SEAT planes are filled with water or a fire suppressant called retardant that they drop at the edge of a fire to keep it from spreading.

SEAT planes are powerhouses! The Forest Service and Bureau of Land Management hire SEAT companies for the summer season to provide the aircraft, pilot, and ground crew.

When the SEAT base is called to go out on fire, they give the pilots a release that has information on where the fire is located. The pilots and crew get the plane ready to go and taxi to the pit to get loaded with retardant. Another crew has the job of mixing the retardant with water and then loading it onto the plane with a big hose that attaches to the belly of the plane and goes into the hopper. The guys call the retardant *mud* for short. It's bright red to dark pink, and according to Mom, it stains my clothes. She even asked whether it was necessary to ride through the puddles. I don't understand why she'd ask a question like that; of course it is!

Anyway, when the day is done, it's time to wash the planes off. The pilots have paperwork to do, so they hand the cleaning responsibility off to the ground crew. The ground crew guys are my friends, and they like it when I stay and help them wash the airplanes. Sometimes I hear the pilot say, "Hope you get more water on the plane than you do you," as he walks away smiling.

The guys usually grin back and reply, "Me too." I think that's one of those inside jokes. I'm not sure, though, because I'm the one with the water hose. The hose is bigger than the ones you have for your yard but smaller than the ones they have on a fire engine. They have quite a bit of pressure, so the mud washes off easily.

Now that I'm older, the guys don't mind if I go in the pits when they aren't really busy. My friend Duane was in education before he retired, so he is always teaching me something new. The way they can tell that they have the mud mixed correctly is with an object called a duo check. The guys all decided I did such a good job learning how they mix the retardant, reading the mixture balance, and washing the plane that they could sit in the shade and watch me do their jobs for them. Funny guys.

This aircraft is a Fire Boss. It's a SEAT plane with amphibious floats. That means that this plane can land on water or a regular runway. It sits up higher than a normal SEAT plane. The super cool thing is that that when it skims the water, it has a hatch that opens up and forces water through a tube into the holding tank. It only takes a few seconds for the plane to get a full load of water, take off, and go to the fire to dump the water. After fire season, many of these SEAT planes go back to working agriculture.

Every summer we get the crew based here, and sometimes they get to come back more than once. They give me their phone numbers, and I can call them and let them know how I'm doing in school. Sometimes when the evenings are nice and there isn't a fire, we all get together and have a barbecue. That's a lot of fun because I get to hear about the different fires they've been on and the experiences they've had.

I like to pull my plane out of the hanger and talk about the cool fire company stickers I've added to my plane since the last time they saw it. My friend Jim

gave me his old prop tether from the plane because he got a new one. Can you guess what that is? A prop tether is a leather sleeve that slides onto a blade of the propeller, and then it has a rope that attaches from the sleeve to the body of the airplane. This keeps the propeller from moving while the plane is parked.

My buddy Parker has the coolest setup in his SEAT plane. He has a hammock! It attaches to the bottom of his airplane, and he can use it to take a nap if he wants. He claims that naps inside, where there's air-conditioning, are better, but he told me I could try it out. It's a great idea in theory, but I might miss out on something if I did fall asleep. Even so, it's still fun to kick back and watch everybody.

The best part about our SEAT base is that they are well supplied with candy and popsicles. Before I leave to go back to the FBO, I fill both pockets up just in case I don't get to see them for a while (you can't very well ride your bike with both hands full, you know). They ask me if I have enough for each pocket. Teamwork is important around here; everyone is always looking out for one another. They think it's pretty funny when Mom says that I'll have to stay down there until the sugar wears off.

My friend Ron flies gliders with the local glider club at the airport. We like to talk about gliders, towing gliders, and flying gliders.

Have you ever looked at a glider up close? They sit lower to the ground than a motorized aircraft. There is a wheel in the middle of the body of the plane and two small wheels on each side of the wingtips. They have those to keep the wings from getting damaged when they tip from one side to the other on the ground. When you are taking the glider out to the launching area and towing it, it helps to have at least one wing walker to keep the wings level.

Speaking of gliders, my best buddy, Jaxon, and I get to go for our first glider ride. Jaxon and I get to go on adventures around this airport quite a bit. We both learned to ride our bikes out on the tarmac, and sometimes his dad takes us both out in his airplane.

Today, Jaxon's dad, Travis, will be flying the tow plane, and our friend Ron will be our pilot in the glider. Gliders are nonpowered airplanes. Some models have a small engine that will get them up in the air, but most need to be towed up in the sky with another airplane. Their wingspan is longer than most planes because wide wings create lift and give stability in flight.

The tow plane is in front of the glider, and the pilots hook up the glider to the tow plane with a rope. Once the tow plane takes off, the glider is behind it. Because the glider is so lightweight, it usually lifts off the ground right before the tow plane. Once the planes get to a selected altitude, the glider can release from the tow plane; then the glider pilot is in complete control of the aircraft. The tow plane makes a low pass to release its end of the rope so that when the plane lands, the rope doesn't drag the ground and wear out quickly. Somebody on the ground retrieves the rope to use again on the next tow. You can get your glider's license at fourteen, and you can get your private pilot's license by sixteen for a motorized aircraft.

If you like to work with your hands and create things, you could build an airplane. Many pilots build their airplane from a kit or from scratch, designing and building each piece of the aircraft. Grandad has several friends who like to build their own airplanes. This is our friend John's airplane, which he built.

I never get bored at the airport; there is always something to do or learn. I finally have Mom convinced I can marshal this small jet that's coming in for the day. She stands behind me and reminds me if I forget the arm motions I'm supposed to make. I wear earplugs, my safety vest, and sunglasses. Marshaling is like being a traffic director who guides the planes to a parking spot; you have brightly colored wands that you use to give signals about where to turn and stop. We don't usually run into tight spots for a plane, but it's good practice to help the jets out anyway. Later, the pilot says I did a good job marshaling him into his parking spot.

My adventures are not just about airplanes and helicopters; I enjoy other kinds of adventures too. I love going to the mountains, fishing, hunting, riding ATVs, and hiking. The adventures are endless. My dad; my half brother, Grady; and I like to explore on the weekends, and sometimes we fly to a remote backcountry strip in the Eagle Cap Wilderness and spend a couple of days exploring the woods. The fishing isn't too bad either! Do you have a favorite place to camp or explore?

The best part of being at the airport is getting to go inside the different helicopters and airplanes. Most of the time, when the pilots aren't busy, they enjoy showing off their aircraft and explaining the different parts and how they work. It's important to be respectful, pay attention to what is going on around you, and be on your best behavior. That's the ticket to getting to see these aircraft up close.

The guys who came in the AirCrane® helicopter let me set in the left seat of the cockpit—that's the pilot's seat. The fire crew who came in for a couple of days with the Chinook helicopter gave me a tour of the inside of their helicopter. In the back, they can haul lots of supplies.

Can you guess what this big orange flag is behind me? It's a windsock. I went with the airport manager, Dan, to put a new one up on the pole. A windsock is cone shaped; it helps pilots to measure the direction of the air and approximate speed the air is traveling. Do you know another name for the movement of air? Wind!

Exciting things are developing at the airport! We are getting a grass runway that will be parallel to the regular runway. This strip will be used by gliders and by most of the planes with big tires. We have to start by taking the old fence down and clearing any old trees and brush that are in the way. Next, some people will come out measure the length and width they need so that a grader can come in and start working the ground to smooth it out.

After that is done, then they'll get a water system in place and sow grass seed. Tail-draggers have friendly little competitions called STOL races. STOL is short for short field takeoff and landing. The pilots practice getting their airplanes off the ground and then landing them again using the shortest distances. It takes mad piloting skills—that's pilot talk for skills and technique. If you get the chance, you can look it up online with your parents. It's fun to watch.

Did you know that even the medical field is involved in aviation? Medical teams can transport the sick and injured to bigger hospitals more efficiently by airplane or helicopter than by ground. Most medevac-type companies have a pilot and a couple of medical personnel who travel together to get patients delivered safely.

Are you ready for tomorrow? That's an important question to ask yourself. I ask myself that question before I go to bed so that I am ready to go the next morning. It keeps me from being rushed and disorganized for school.

It's also a question that I ask when something exciting is going to happen the next day—like Aviation Field Day. Every year kids in junior high from our county get to spend a day at the airport, learning about different careers that involve aviation in some way. It starts with an early-morning arrival at the airport for the volunteers teaching a station and helping with the field day. Everyone gets coffee and doughnuts except for me—I get hot chocolate and two doughnuts.

The students are put into small groups with a leader. Throughout the day, students go to every station and learn something new. They hear about humanitarian services that provide for the needs of people in remote areas all around the world using aircraft, and they learn about the principles of flight, which is how an airplane flies, and about aviation mechanics.

Avionics are the pieces of electronic equipment used to operate an aircraft, and they are important in aviation. Some pilots take out all their old aviation equipment and have it replaced with a glass panel, which is pretty much a computer for the dashboard of the plane.

One of my favorite stations is the one where students get to sit inside a corporate jet and talk to the pilot. Corporate pilots take their clients into airports all around the world on the schedule of the client. Most of the time, they travel for business, but sometimes the passengers are going on vacation. During the fall, we get jets that come in with hunters.

Remember when I said that there were humanitarian needs that are served by the aviation industry? The Mission Aviation Fellowship (MAF) is just a little way from our airport. MAF airplanes fly over jungles, deserts, and mountains to reach faraway villages all around the world. Sometimes the airplanes have floats on them so they can land on rivers and lakes. The airplanes are carrying doctors, nurses, and missionaries to the villages. They bring medical supplies, food, and Bibles that talk about Jesus. The MAF brings their push plane, *Petey*, for students to see and to pose for pictures.

I've been learning parts of the airplane for a long time, and now I get to pass on what I've learned to someone else. It is exciting to share aviation with others, and I hope they like learning about what makes planes fly, even if I am younger than they are.

I hope you had fun learning a little about what happens at a small airport. It's a great place to experience real-life adventures and see how much science, technology, engineering, and math affect everyday life in aviation. The cool thing about being around what you love to do is that every day you get the opportunity to learn something new or to practice what you already know to grow the skills you have. Stay focused, aim for purpose, and don't forget my favorite question: Are you ready for tomorrow?

Your buddy,
Cash Troyer

ACKNOWLEDGMENT

From the time Cash was a little guy, he had an incredible sense of direction and was a natural born navigator. He had a genuine interest and curiosity about all aspects of aviation and loved meeting the many different pilots who traveled through over the years.

This book is inspired by my precious boy's love of aviation but also the SEAT pilots, ground crews, and tanker base manager, Brian. You guys had such a profound effect on Cash's life; he adored you all. Gene Sullivan, he was determined to be in the seat beside you to fly around the world one day. Thank you for inspiring him to dream big. Dan, thank you for allowing him to tag along on daily tasks around the airport and the grass strip project. He was convinced he should be able to skip school because he was learning so much working beside you. Marisa and Richann, thank you for being the educators who didn't mind indulging a little boy's imagination and dreams and his nonstop plane talk and stories. Barb and Nickie, thank you for including him in so many projects and experiments. He would be so proud to be honored by those national awards. Jaxon and Kirk, the one-of-a-kind best friends who would bless any boy. To our family, who all had a lasting impression on Cash. Remington and Karrington, you might have bossed him around more than he cared for, but he loved his sisters fiercely. Finally, to the granddad who inspired and promoted his love of aviation.

Printed in the United States
By Bookmasters